Copyright Notice

Munich's Ten G⸺
Your Local Companion to the Greatest Places

Copyright © 2013 Marion Kummerow, www.inside-munich.com
Weißtannenweg 7
80939 Munich, Germany

This book is copyrighted and protected by copyright laws.

„To get more tips about Munich and Germany, click the link below to subscribe to our newsletter."
http://inside-munich.com/chrtips

No part of this publication may be reproduced or transmitted in any form or by any means, electronic, mechanical, photocopying, recording, or otherwise without the prior written permission from the author.

All maps are copyright © OpenStreetMap contributors
http://www.openstreetmap.org/copyright

This publication contains the author's opinions and ideas. It's for informative purposes only and is not intended as professional advice.

The author has used her best efforts in writing this book and the accompanying materials. The author makes no representation or warranties of any kind with respect to the completeness, accuracy, or applicability of the contents of the book.
The author specifically disclaims any responsibility for any liability, loss or risk, personal or otherwise, caused or alleged to be caused, directly or indirectly by using any information described in this publication.

Table of Contents

1. Introduction 3
2. Marienplatz 6
3. Viktualienmarkt 12
4. Englischer Garten / English Garden 14
5. Frauenkirche 21
6. Odeonsplatz 25
7. Königsplatz 31
8. Kunstareal: Pinakotheken 36
9. Olmypiapark 42
10. BMW Experience Park 46
11. Nymphenburg Castle 50
12. About the Author 55

1   Introduction

Munich has hundreds of attractions, and to fully appreciate everything this city has to offer, you would need to stay here weeks and maybe months.
However, I boiled down the many attractions to the **10 Gorgeous Gems**, the ones you absolutely must visit.

Each of these 10 must-see sights could keep you busy for an entire day. But I know you have a limited amount of time in our wonderful city and need to make the most of it, and still not miss any of the greatest attractions.

Therefore, I have included for your convenience three different itineraries with each of the Gorgeous Gems, which suggest what to do when you're on a short, medium or long time budget.

Short means you can do all the 10 star attractions in as little as one day. Medium will take you two days and long at least three days to visit them all. Of course, you can mix and match according to your interests and spend more time at the attraction that interests you most, while only superficially visiting the others.

If you're on an extra-short itinerary because you have only six to eight hours of stopover at the Munich airport, I have a special "fast-track" tip for you.
The attractions are in order to make it easiest to see everything with the least amount of time for traveling from one highlight to the next. This is especially important for short itineraries. On longer stays you can easily change the order as you like and focus on certain areas on different days.

Even before arriving in Munich, you can optimize your trip by choosing the right days to be here. This is especially true if you have only one day. With this guide book you won't have to regret that you missed the best spots, ran out of time or arrived at the museum just when it was about to close.

You'll find detailed information about opening and closing hours and days for each of the Gorgeous Gems within their chapters. You want to make sure you get to see what you want without worrying about the hours it opens or closes.

1.1   Cost-Saving Tips

State-Owned Castles

Even if you plan to tour just the two castles in this guide (Residenz and Nymphenburg), you can save on admission fees by buying a 14-day pass.

The 14-day pass is valid for two weeks from your first visit, and you can use it in more than 40 state-owned attractions in Bavaria. If you plan to visit Neuschwanstein as well, this pass is a no-brainer.

The 14-day ticket costs 24 Euro for one adult and 40 Euro for a family, and you can buy it at the ticket desk of any of the participating attractions.

Read all the details here:
http://inside-munich.com/gems-14pass

State- and City-Owned Museums
Sunday is 1 Euro Day.
All state- and city-owned museums in Munich cost an admission fee of only 1 Euro on Sundays. If you want to take advantage of this price, come early because the museums tend to fill up in the afternoon.

Public transport and museums
If you need public transport and plan to enter several of the highlights in Munich, then you can buy a *citytourcard*. It offers unlimited use of the public transport during one or three days as well as discounts in many attractions.
You can buy it at one of the self-service machines in any underground or S-Bahn station.
Prices:
One day: 1 Person 9,90 Euro up to 5 people 17,90 Euro
3 days: 1 Person 20,90 Euro up to 5 people 30,90 Euro

See all the details here:
http://www.citytourcard-muenchen.com/

Public Transport

Public transport in Munich is excellent. Underground, S-bahn, trams and buses run frequently and take you anywhere. All of the Gorgeous Gems in this book are within the Innenraum, that is, the inner white circle on the public transport maps.

You can download the public transport map here (it is essential if you plan to get around a lot by underground):
http://inside-munich.com/gem-ubahn

Prices:
One-day ticket: 6 Euro single 11,20 Euro partner (up to 5 people)
3-day-ticket : 15 Euro single and 25,90 Euro partner

Weekly or monthly ticket: This is your choice if you stay one week or longer. Buy rings 1 to 4, that equals the Innenraum. Since December 2013 the weekly or monthly tickets can start any day of the week or month.

Prices:
Weekly 4 Rings (Innenraum): 19,60 Euro
Monthly 4 Rings (Innenraum): 71,50 Euro

1.2 Time-Saving Tip

If you absolutely must see everything mentioned in this guide within four to six hours, take a Hop-on Hop-off Tour. Make sure, to take the Grand Tour, though, because the Express Tour won't take you all the way to Nymphenburg Castle and the Olympiapark/BMW Experience Park.

The tours start just across Hauptbahnhof in front of the Karstadt shopping center, but you can also board at any of the stops. You can't miss the blue, red or yellow open air double-decker buses. The buses run every 20 to 30 minutes from 9 a.m. to 6 p.m. and cost 19 Euro for the Grand Tour.
The non-stop tour takes two-and-a-half hours. But you can use the buses for up to 24 hours and get off and on again as many times as you want.
If you wish to book your tickets in advance, you can do so here:
http://inside-munich.com/gems-hop-on

1.3 Extra Planning Tip

Most museums close on Mondays, so make sure to organize your trip in a way that doesn't include a Monday. This is especially true if you're here for only one day!
Shopping fans need to keep in mind that all shops (except gas stations and some shops at Central Station) close on Sundays and holidays.
Christmas is a fantastic time to visit Munich and experience the wonderful Christmas markets, but from December 24 through 26 basically everything closes in Germany. This even includes most of the restaurants.

2 Marienplatz

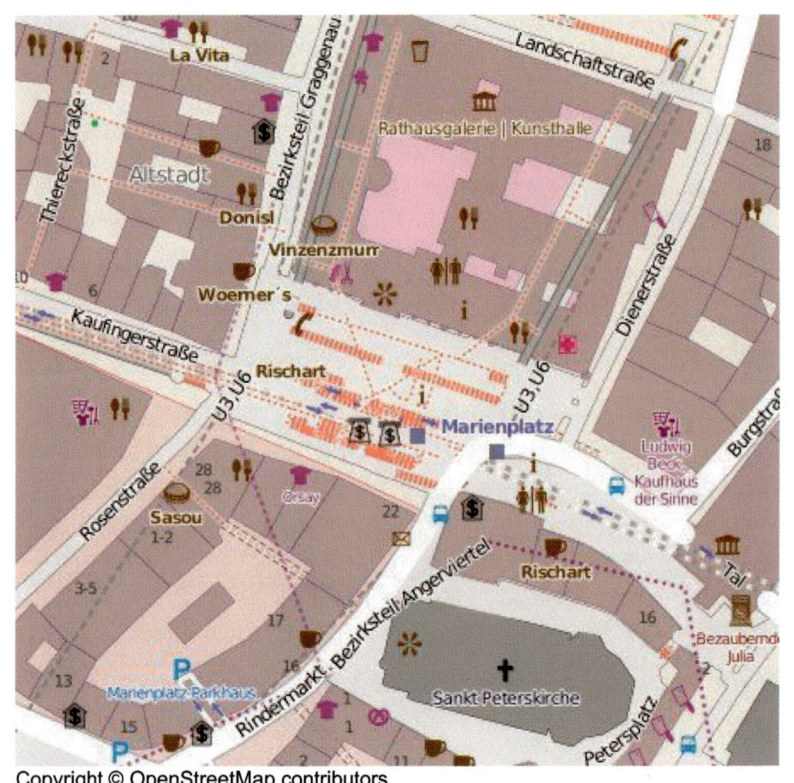

Copyright © OpenStreetMap contributors

Marienplatz is the center of Munich, not only of the historical Old Town but also of the modern city, lying prominently amidst the main shopping streets.If you haven't seen Marienplatz, you haven't seen Munich. It's the best starting point for any sightseeing tour and if there's nothing else you can visit, this is the place to go.

The big square is usually bustling with crowds visiting the different attractions, watching and listening to the Glockenspiel, shopping, eating and drinking in one of the restaurants with outside seating areas, waiting for friends to meet, etc.

The tourist office is in one of the Neues Rathaus arcades. They offer anything and everything about Munich and also sell tickets to most events.

2.1 Neues Rathaus

The Neues Rathaus (New Town Hall) sits at the north end of Marienplatz. It's a huge and impressive neo-gothic building from the late 1800s. The city uses the word "new" because it replaced the much older old town house in 1874.

Georg von Hauberrisser built it as the mayor's office between 1867 and 1874. Nowadays, it houses the mayor's office, the city council and the headquarters of the city administration.

Fantastic ornaments richly decorate many of the rooms and sightseers can visit some of the rooms. Even the mayor's office is open to visitors once a year during the "Day of Open Doors."
If you have a chance, go inside and stroll through the open public halls.

Extra Tip
The Town Hall Tower is accessible weekdays from 10 a.m. to 5 p.m. (in summer 10 a.m. to 7 p.m.) and offers a spectacular view over the city center and even as far as the Alps, weather permitting.
Admittedly, the view from the Alter Peter is even more magnificent. The Town Hall Tower, though, has the advantage of accessibility via lift (elevator). No need to climb hundreds of stairs.

2.2 Altes Rathaus

The Old Town Hall marks the east end of Marienplatz and was the town hall from the 14th century until 1874, when the city administration moved to the Neues Rathaus.

The facade is rather simple and unostentatious, but the interior is impressive, especially the gothic festival hall that's used today as a representative room for mayoral events.

In earlier days the building was solid from ground to top, but when the city council moved to the New Town Hall, a big arcade replaced the ground floor and is now a passageway for cars and pedestrians from Marienplatz to the adjoining street Im Tal.

Today, the building houses (besides the state rooms) the toys museum, which is a great place to go with kids.

Hours (Toys Museum)
Daily 10 a.m. to 5.30 p.m.

Admission Fee
Adults   4 Euro
Kids   1 Euro

2.3   Glockenspiel – Carillion

Probably the Glockenspiel is the most famous tourist attraction in Munich. The Glockenspiel or Carillion plays every day at 11 a.m. and noon (in summer at 5 p.m. also). Thousands gather in front of the Neues Rathaus to watch the spectacle.

The figurines represent two stories from Munich's past:

1. The upper story shows the wedding of Duke Wilhelm V with Renate von Lothringen (Lorraine) in 1568. In honor to the bridal couple there was a knight's tournament at the Marienplatz.

2. The lower story shows the so-called Schäfflertanz (dance of the coopers). According to the legend the coopers were the first ones to go out into the streets after a very bad outburst of the Black Death. They started dancing to cheer up the population that had survived the plague.

And there's another little-known spectacle every day at 9 p.m. The Münchner Kindl resides on top of the tower and watches over the city of Munich. Münchner Kindl means "Munich child" and is the name of the official symbol on the coat of arms.

Like every kid it has to go bed at night. At 9 p.m. a night watchman appears in the oriel of the seventh floor and blows his horn with music from Richard Wagner's *Die Meistersinger von Nürnberg*. The Münchner Kindl follows him and finally, the angel of peace with the *Wiegenlied* (Brahm's lullaby) by Johannes Brahms.

2.4 Pedestrian Shopping Area

Marienplatz is also the center of Munich's main shopping area. To the north on either side of the Neues Rathaus are Weinstrasse and Dienerstrasse, two bustling shopping streets.

On the Dienerstrasse you find the famous Dallmayer's Delikatessen with the best German and International delicacies. To the west the Kaufingerstrasse leads to Karlsplatz/Stachus. This is the biggest shopping street in Munich and commonly referred to as *Fussgängerzone* (pedestrian area) or *Stadt* (city).

To the south is the Rosenstrasse that leads into Sendlinger Strasse until Sendlinger Tor. This is another great shopping street that's less crowded than Kaufingerstrasse.
To the east is Im Tal that leads all the way up to Isartor. Still a great place to shop, but less relaxing, because this street has car traffic, while the others are pedestrian zones. (Sendlinger Strasse is partly open for traffic, though.)

Extra Tip
Stock up on English books and travel guides at Hugendubel, Munich's biggest bookstore right at the corner of Marienplatz. They have lots of comfortable sofas to sit down and browse through the books you're interested in.

2.5 Alter Peter

The Church of St. Peter, the official name, is the oldest parish church in Munich. First constructed in the 11th century, it has been rebuilt many times. It stands on the only (though small) hill of Munich's city center, called Petersbergl (Peter's little mountain).

Inside the church are some fantastic pieces of artwork such as a gilded high altar from the 18th century and large ceiling frescoes that extend along the entire nave.

Another exhibition is the shrine for relics of the Holy Munditia. She lived around 250 A.D. and was in the Roman catacombs. St Peter's received her skeleton as a gift in the 17th century.

From the tower you have the most impressive panoramic view of the historical center. In good weather you can see quite a bit of the Alps, a stunning sight you shouldn't miss. Unfortunately there is some sweaty work involved: You must climb 299 stairs to reach the platform.

The tower features some of the oldest bells in Munich. They were made as early as 1327. The oldest and smallest bell in the tower that you can see when climbing the stairs is the Arme-Sünder-Glocke (Poor sinners bell). It used to ring during one of the frequent executions on Marienplatz during Medieval times.

Hours
Daily from 9 a.m. (10 a.m. on weekends) to 6 p.m. in winter and 7 p.m. in summer.

Admission Fee
Adults 1,50 Euro
Kids (6 and older) and students 1 Euro

2.6 Meeting Spots and How to Get There

There are two main spots to meet: either the Fischbrunnen (fish fountain) on the east end of Marienplatz or the Mariensäule (Maria statue) on the west end. Both spots are perfect. You just can't miss anyone waiting there.

All S-Bahn lines and the underground lines 3 and 6 stop at Marienplatz station. You can't miss it.

2.7 Places to Eat

Keep in mind that Marienplatz is the most touristy place in Munich. Prices are higher than elsewhere, and the chance to fall into a tourist trap is even bigger. With that in mind I have two recommendations for you:

Café Glockenspiel
The cafe is on the top floor in a building at the south end of Marienplatz. The entrance is slightly hidden in the back building at Rosenstrasse. Go there for brunch and take a table at the big window front overlooking the Marienplatz. Here's your prime spot to watch the Glockenspiel close up. It's definitely the best place to watch the Glockenspiel. The breakfast is fantastic, too, but this is also a nice place for some cocktails at night.

Rathauskeller
This might well be the biggest restaurant in Munich. It's located beneath the Neues Rathaus and is huge. Go down there and pray that you'll find your way out again (just kidding). Each room has different decorations, but all of them give that warm cozy Bavarian gemütlichkeit (friendliness). Also, there's great food and beer.

2.8 Itineraries

Short: Wander around Marienplatz and view the picturesque buildings. If you're here when the Glockenspiel plays, take the time to watch the spectacle.

Medium: Enter the Town Hall to visit some of the publicly open historical rooms and the hall. Climb either the Town Hall tower or the Alter Peter to have a panoramic view of Munich.

Long: Brunch at Café Glockenspiel, visit Alter Peter Church and do some shopping or visit the toy museum.

3   Viktualienmarkt

Copyright © OpenStreetMap contributors

The Viktualienmarkt is Munich's oldest food market. It has been at Marienplatz since the beginnings of the city and moved to its current location in 1807 because it became too big. Here you can buy fresh fruits, veggies, cheese, sausages and any other delicatessen food you can think of.

Apart from the famous Dallmayr Delikatessen (the one with the spectacular coffee) at Marienplatz this is the place to go for any fresh or exotic food.
If you like food shopping, you'll love the Viktualienmarket. It's open air and hosts more than 140 different stalls, each one specializing in a different food.

There's probably nothing you can't get: wine, cheese, honey, exotic fruits, bread, sausages, flowers, meat, arts and crafts, you name it. There even are two stalls with fresh fish, which are probably the only places in Munich where you can get really fresh saltwater fish (remember Munich is a few hundred kilometers from the nearest ocean).

Just to warn you, Viktualienmarkt is not cheap: the things you can buy here are of best quality, often rare, and rare has its price.

3.1 Beer Garden

Apart from the market, there's one more reason to visit the Viktualienmarkt: A beer garden sits prominently in the middle of the big square.

It may not be the nicest and most romantic of Munich's beer gardens, but it's right there when you need it after some strenuous shopping or sightseeing. This is the perfect place to sit down and relax with a cold beer or Radler (beer mixed with lemonade) in the middle of Munich.

3.2 Meeting Spot and How to Get There

Meet at the center of Viktualienmarkt beneath the big maypole. If you have to wait longer, meet directly at the beer garden. It's not too big so you can find each other, and you can have your first cold beer while waiting.
Walk five minutes from Marienplatz.

3.3 Places to Eat

Everywhere! If you want to sit down, go to the beer garden. Another nice place (but not typical) is the Nordsee, a kind of seafood fast food.

3.4 Itineraries

Short: Walk across Viktualienmarkt and buy a thing or two. If you're hungry, a Leberkässemmel (meatloaf with finely ground corned beef, pork, bacon, liver and onions) or a bratwurst to take away will do the trick.

Medium: Have a break at the beer garden.

Long: Take a guided tour, including the tasting of some local delicacies and lots of historical information.

4   Englischer Garten / English Garden

Copyright © OpenStreetMap contributors

The English Garden lies in the center of Munich, and with its 373 hectares (900 acres), it's not only Munich's biggest recreational area but also one of the biggest urban parks worldwide, even larger than New York's Central Park.

Munich residents love the English Garden, and you'll never be completely alone there. There are many things to see inside the park so I'll just name the most important attractions.

The English Garden is so big I had problems fitting everything into the little map above. Please follow the link below for a more detailed map with exact locations of the mentioned attractions.
www.inside-munich.com/map

4.1 The Park

The English Garden is huge and stretches from the center of the city (near Odeonsplatz) to the northern city border. You can't see everything in one day or even in one week.

It's divided into two sections: The southern part (Südteil) near the city and the northern section (Nordteil), both parts separated by Mittlerer Ring Street and connected via pedestrian bridges.

While the southern part contains all the sights and is pretty crowded, the northern part is less busy. It's the place to go when you want peace and quiet. You can walk or bike virtually for hours and enjoy wonderful days here, including a visit to three wonderful beer gardens.

Elector Karl Theodor first opened the park in 1789. Originally, he reserved it for the army troops' recreation, but just three years later, he opened it to the general public, as well. The British landscaper Benjamin Thompson (who would become Count Rumford later on) and Friedrich Ludwig von Sckell designed it. The park has the name "Englischer Garten" because the designers created it in the style of an English park and not like the then-modern French baroque parks.

You can swim in any of the creeks in the Englischer Garten, but be careful. The current is strong and dangerous. Swim only where you see lots of locals (and not only adventurous teenagers).

The English Garden is also home to five beer gardens: Chinesischer Turm, Seehaus, Hirschau, Aumeister, and Mini Hofbräuhaus. The Chinese Tower is the most popular one.

4.2 Monopteros

Don't miss the Monopteros. It's in the southern part of the park, and you can see it from far away.

King Ludwig I commissioned Leo von Klenze in the second half of the 19th century to erect this little temple in a Greek style. By itself, it's not a really interesting sight, the view from there, however, is simply stunning.

Climb up the hill to this Greek-looking monument, and you can enjoy a terrific view of the English garden and Munich's skyline. On a clear day with "Föhn" (a warm wind from Italy), you can even see as far as the Alps.

In winter, this is a popular sledding hill for the little ones. In summer sunbathers flock to the greens around it to enjoy the sun. Be prepared to see nude sunbathers. Since the 1960s, the area between the Monopteros and the Eisbach (one of three icy creeks in the English Garden), has become the "official" nude bathing spot.

4.3 Chinesischer Turm ✳

The Chinesischer Turm (Chinese Tower) is a 25-meter-high (a little more than 82 feet) wooden structure resembling the pagodas of the Chinese emperors and the central sight in Munich's biggest beer garden, which has more than 7000 seats. Whenever you take a stroll through the park, this beer garden is almost impossible to miss.

It's a polygonal structure with five stories. The tower's diameter is 19 meters (about 62.5 feet) at ground level and about six meters (nearly 20 feet) in the highest story. You can pass beneath the structure at ground level, but unfortunately, you can only climb the stairs inside during special events. Normally, it's closed to visitors.

Almost everyone in Munich knows and likes the Chinesischer Turm beer garden. Even though it's now a big tourist attraction, you still meet many locals here. Many visitors are students from the nearby University of Munich (LMU).

The Chinesischer Turm beer garden is equipped with **wireless Internet access,** and you can quickly meet up with people or let your friends know you're relaxing in the shadow beneath the chestnut trees drinking a beer and eating a Brezn.

It's also is one of the few beer gardens that has live, traditional Bavarian music every weekend and many times during the week in summer – definitely something you shouldn't miss.

Apart from the self-service beer garden, you can choose to eat in the restaurant Chinesischer Turm, which has a really nice atmosphere.

Another big event held at the Chinese tower beer garden is the Christmas mart, which is said to be the second biggest one in Munich (after Marienplatz). In my opinion, it's definitely the coldest Christmas market, because it lacks big buildings to protect you from the icy winds.

4.4   Kleinhesseloher See and Seehaus Beer Garden

The Kleinhesseloher See is a small lake in the English Garden. Unfortunately, it's not suitable for swimming or even bathing your feet. This is because it's very shallow and home to a myriad of ducks and swans. Therefore, the water is quite dirty and muddy.

But there's one fun activity you can do on the lake: rent a pedal boat and pedal around the lake. The landing stage for pedal boats is just a few meters from Seehaus beer garden. You can rent the boats for half an hour or a full hour. Given the size of the lake, half an hour is more than enough. This is especially fun if you have children.

After your sports activity, take a break and have a beer, Radler or Apfelschorle (apple juice with sparkling water) at the Seehaus beer garden. This is a really nice beer garden where you can sit on the lakeshore. It also features a fenced-in playground where you can leave your kids and a fancy restaurant for the cooler days.

We like to take a walk around the lake (about half an hour) in the shade of the trees. A wonderful contrast to the otherwise busy life in Munich.

4.5 Eisbach Surfers

Despite being a landlocked city hundreds of miles from the nearest beach, Munich is still known as a hotspot for surfing. Come to the Eisbach (icy creek) and see for yourself!

The standing wave at the Eisbach has become a symbol for the city that almost every tourist and local has watched at least once. And it's a lot of fun to watch. Mind you, this is a year-round activity.

We recently went in early January, and there they were: surfers dressed in neoprene suits, hats, gloves, and shoes defying the cold outside temperatures of just above 0°C/32°F and the similarly cold water.

The wave is only for experts. Don't even think of trying it yourself!
The Eisbach is very dangerous. Even though farther down the waterway people swim, it's not recommended! Every year a few people die when swimming here. Don't do it!

The current is fast, strong, and treacherous, the wave even more so, partly due to flow-breaking concrete rocks in the riverbed. I recommend you watch the surfers and have fun but get in the water only if you're already an expert. **No beginners here!**

The Eisbach wave is very purposely located between the two museums, the Bavarian National Museum and Haus der Kunst. After a tiring museum visit, you can stroll over to the bridge and join the other spectators in this refreshing activity.

4.6　Kocherlball

The Kocherlball dates to the 19th century. Around 1880, the working servants in Munich started to meet every Sunday in summer very early in the morning at the Chinesischer Turm to dance and have fun. And that's exactly what this festival is all about. :-)
It must be one of the most peculiar dancing events in the world.
It takes place only once a year (on the 3rd Sunday in July) at 6:00 a.m. Thousands of people flock to Chinesischer Turm as early as 2:00 or 3:00 a.m. to secure the best places.

Yes, I know, this is early! But it's worth it: People either dress up in old-fashioned clothes or put on their finest dirndls and lederhosen. An orchestra plays polkas and other traditional dances. There's even a "dance master" who teaches novices a few of the steps so everyone can join in and have fun.

Once the event ends at 10 a.m., you have the rest of the day to enjoy the Englischer Garten.

4.7　Japanisches Teehaus

The Japanese Teahouse is something you might not expect in a German city. Dr. Soshitsu Sen from the Ursaenke Tea School in Kyoto, Japan donated it to the state of Bavaria on the occasion of the Olympic Games in Munich 1972. Since then, there are instructors who teach and present the original Japanese tea ceremony.
It's located on a small island behind the Haus der Kunst at the very south end of the English Garden (near the Eisbach surfers).

Hours
Presentations are usually every weekend from April to October and last about one hour. Make sure to check the current timetable at their website:
http://www.urasenke-muenchen.de/

Admission Fee
Adults	6 Euro
Kids under 12 years	3 Euro

Tea and a small sweet are included in the admission.

4.8 Meeting Spots and How to Get There

There are a few places to meet, depending on where you enter the park.

North: Coming from U6/U3 Giselastrasse. Take the bus and exit at the bus station "Chinesischer Turm." The entrance to the beer garden is right beside the bus station, so it's the perfect meeting spot if you want to explore Kleinhesseloher See, Chinesischer Turm, and Monopteros.

West: Coming from U6/U3 Universität meet at the "Milchhäusl" kiosk, right at the entrance to Englischer Garten. You can't miss the gondolas, which come from a cable car for skiing in the Alps.

South: Coming from the city or one of the museums on Prinzregentenstrasse, wait at the Eisbach bridge and watch the surfers while you wait for your friends.

4.9 Places to Eat

The obvious place is one of the beer gardens. For tourists, the most appropriate (because they're in the southern part near the city) are Chinesischer Turm and Seehaus. But you can also buy a take-away snack at the Milchäusl.

4.10 Itineraries

Short: Take the bus to Chinesischer Turm and head straight to the beer garden. Admire the Chinese Tower, while enjoying a beer and a Brezn.

Medium: Start at Haus der Kunst, watch the Eisbach surfer, walk by the Japanisches Teehaus up to the Monopterus and the Chinese Tower. Stay here for a cold beer or Radler.

Long: This is best done by bike. Include the Kleinhesseloher Lake and the Seehaus beer garden in your tour. Take a trip to the north part and visit the Aumeister beer garden. Walk or bike along the Isar River. You might even want to stick your feet in the water from the gravel banks if the day is hot.

5   Frauenkirche   ✳

Copyright © OpenStreetMap contributors

The Frauenkirche is Munich's main landmark. The official name is Dom zu unserer lieben Frau, or Cathedral Church of Our Lady.

You feel and see its presence almost anywhere in Munich. There even is a law that forbids any other building to be higher than the Frauenkirche for fear it would ruin the skyline. Some skyscrapers at the city limits are exceptions because they were built before the law passed.

Construction began in 1468 under architect Jörg von Halsbach, who Prince Sigismund commissioned. The builders completed the legendary towers with the onion domes 20 years later in 1488. The Roman Catholic Church consecrated the cathedral in 1494.

During World War II the Frauenkirche received heavy damage from air strikes, and only one of the towers remained. Some say that the suffering population saw this as a miracle. They felt that if one of the towers could survive, they also could recover from the war's hardships.

Later on, the Frauenkirche returned to its original glory and officially opened almost 50 years later in 1994.

Hours
Saturday through Wednesday from 7 a.m. to 7 p.m.
Thursday 7 a.m. to 8:30 p.m.
Friday 7 a.m. to 6 p.m.

Admission is free.

5.1 The Twin Onion Domes

People usually can climb the south tower and have excellent views of the city. Unfortunately, it's not open due to construction work, and according to the mayor's office, it will not reopen until 2016.

If you want panoramic views, climb the Alter Peter or the Town Hall Tower at Marienplatz.

By the way, it's an urban myth that the north tower is about one meter higher than the south tower. It just looks like that. But according to the city of Munich the twin towers measure 98.57 meters and 98.45 meters, which makes a difference of only 12 cm (five inches).

5.2 Devil's Footprint

It isn't just the outside that's striking. The interior is vast and filled with the entire splendor you would expect in a cathedral. When you walk in, the threshold is of particular note.

In the entrance of this imposing late-Gothic interior you encounter among other things the legendary devil's footprint in the floor of the church.

See for yourself and put your foot in the footprint. All the windows are behind the columns.

According to the legend, the architect made a deal with the devil: The devil helped him build the church in exchange for the architect Jörg Ganghofer's soul. But the cunning architect led the devil to this exact point and refused to hand over his soul, arguing that the devil had botched the construction.

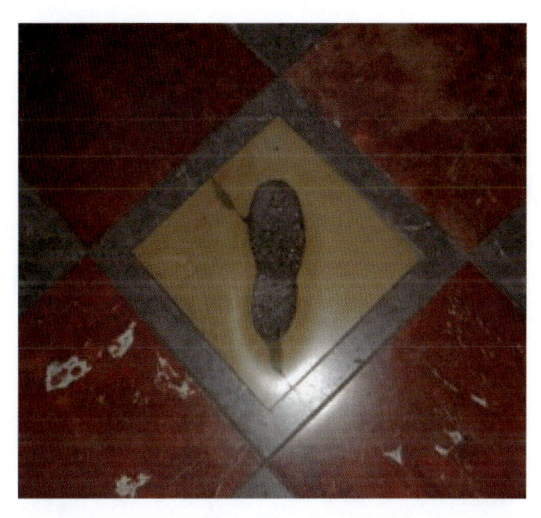

The devil was so furious that he stomped with his foot and left the footprint. Since then he's flying around the church as wind. And when you enter the Frauenkirche, you will notice there really is a soft wind all the time.

5.3 Choir and Organ Concerts

One of the most impressive events is to listen to an organ concert in the Frauenkirche. In August there's an organ concert every Saturday at noon, and it's free. Also, the Frauenkirche is home to a few choirs that regularly have concerts.

The best place to get information about scheduled organ or choir concerts is the tourist office.

5.4 Crypt and Cenotaph

When entering the church through the main portal you see a big, dark casket to the right. This is a cenotaph, an empty grave for Kaiser Ludwig of Bavaria. His remains are in the crypt.

The crypt, built in 1971 during the reconstruction of the WW II-damaged church, lies beneath the cathedral. . An inscription at the entrance wall remembers the Wittelsbacher family who are buried here.

Among them are the Holy Roman Emperor Ludwig the Bavarian (1292 – 1347) and Duke Wilhelm IV of Bavaria (1493 –1550).

5.5 Meeting Spot and How to Get There

A great meeting spot is in on the square just opposite the entrance portal. It's relaxing during the day and romantic at night when the little fountains sparkle with lights.

You can sit near the water on the stone stairs and take in the stunning sight for a while before entering the church. Walking: Just a short walk from Marienplatz

5.6 Places to Eat

There are quite a few restaurants around the cathedral. One of the most traditional and gemütlich (pleasant, agreeable) places is the **Bratwurst Glöckl**. First mentioned in 1390, it's even older than the Frauenkirche itself.

The house specialty is Nuremberg Bratwurst (sausage) that the restaurant makes fresh every day and grills over the open fire barbecue.

5.7 Itineraries

Short: Enjoy the stunning sight and then enter the church for a short walk through it.

Medium: Sit and relax near the water, write postcards. Visit the crypt.

Long: Take a guided tour and listen to an organ concert, if possible.

6 Odeonsplatz

Copyright © OpenStreetMap contributors

Odeonsplatz is a huge square in the center of Munich that you definitely should see. Quite a few attractions surround the square.

6.1 Feldherrnhalle

On the southern border of Odeonsplatz is the Feldherrnhalle. King Ludwig I (not to be confused with Ludwig II, the fairy tale king) built it from 1841 to 1844 in honor of the Bavarian army.

During the National Socialism period (1933 – 1945) it became an important place for the Nazis.

They erected a memorial, where everyone had to give the Hitler salute (Hitlergruss). People from Munich are astute so they found a way to avoid this by entering the square through the small Viscardigasse without having to pass the memorial.

Due to this the residents affectionately call the lane *Drückebergergasserl* (slacker lane). Today, you can see a golden flag on the ground as a memory to the silent protest.

The Feldherrnhalle also marks the beginning of the Ludwigstrasse, the big street to the north that merges into Leopoldstrasse.

6.2 Theatinerkirche

To the west of the square you find the very impressive Theatinerkirche (Theatiner Church), also called St. Kajetan. The full name is Theatine Church of St. Kajetan. It's a Roman Catholic church; many say the most beautiful one in Munich. With its bright yellow color, you can't miss it.

Henriette Adelheid von Savoyen commissioned it in 1662 as a thank you to God for the birth of her son Elector (Kurfürst) Max Emmanuel.

Inspired by the Italian church Sant'Andrea della Valle in Rome and Italian architect Agostino Barelli designed it. The facade is in Rococo style, but the interior is Italian Baroque.

The facade remained incomplete until more than a hundred years later, François de Cuvilliés, who also built the Cuvilliés Theater, finished it. The theater lies just across the street inside the Residenz palace.

You may find the completely white interior even more impressive than the yellow façade. Built in the 17th century in the Italian high-Baroque style, many consider it one of the most outstanding examples of Baroque architecture in all of Europe.

Next to Theatine Church is a Dominican cloister. The monks still live, work and pray here. Therefore, you cannot visit the cloister, but you can oftentimes see the monks in the church.

As in the Frauenkirche, there are many organ concerts, and if you have the time, you should definitely listen to one of those uplifting musical events. You can find a complete schedule of events on the website of the Theatinerkirche:
http://www.theatinerkirche.de

From the beginning it also served as a burial place for the royal Wittelsbach family. In the Fürstengruft (crypt) 47 members of the royal family are buried in metal coffins. A small chapel in the main church contains the tombs of King Maximilian II and his wife Queen Marie.

Hours for the Crypt
Daily 10 a.m. to 1:30 p.m. and 2 p.m. to 4:30 p.m.

Admission Fee for the Crypt
2 Euro

6.3   Bavarian Ministries and Wittelsbacher Platz

Further north, but still on the west side of Odeonsplatz is the Bavarian Ministry of the Interior. It resides in a majestic building the famous Munich architect Leo von Klenze built. The Odeon (concert hall) is on the southwestern side and is no longer a concert hall but part of the ministry.

The next building is the Palais Leuchtenberg, home of the Bavarian Finance Ministry. In front of the building you see a statue of King Ludwig I on his horse.

Just a few steps farther (walk the small street between the two Ministry buildings) is the Wittelsbacher Platz. It features an equally impressive statue of Kurfürst Maximilian I on his horse. At the north end of the square you see the pink Palais Ferdinand that today contains the world headquarters of the Siemens Company.

During December the Wittelsbacher Platz has one very special attraction: a medieval Christmas market.

6.4 Residenz

The Residenz is one of the biggest attractions in Munich. Its sheer size will impress you. It used to be the royal palace of the Wittelsbacher monarchy. It's by far the largest city palace in Germany, and you could spend an entire week seeing everything.

Construction of the whole palace lasted for several centuries. It started in 1385 under Duke Stephan III with the Neuveste. Slowly, more and more buildings and courtyards were added up to the 16th century.

In 1571 the Antiquarium was built as a representative hall to host the royal collection of antique sculptures. The Antiquarium is still one of the highlights of every tour. The court garden (Hofgarten) was laid out in 1613. And the last addition to the complex was the Old Treasury in 1897.

If you're interested in the complete history of the Residenz, you can find plenty of useful information (including a leaflet with a map and description of the most important rooms) at the official website:
http://www.residenz-muenchen.de

The outside is stunning by itself. Take the time to walk around the impressive building, enter the patio and take a short walk in the park-like Hofgarten. The Hofgarten has a direct connection to the English Garden.

The Residenz Museum is the heart and center of the compound. If you have the time, take a tour through the more than 130 richly decorated rooms. If you have even more time, visit the Schatzkammer (treasury) that exhibits the crown jewels of the Bavarian kings, the red and golden Cuvilliés Theater in rococo style and the Egyptian museum.

Don't forget to rub all the four bronze lions, lined up alongside the Residenz Strasse. Rubbing the lion's noses is supposed to bring you luck. :-)

Note:
The Residenz is a very old and big palace, and restoration work is continuous so not all rooms or attractions are open at all times.

Hours
April – mid-October: Daily 9 a.m. to 6 p.m.
Mid-October – March: Daily 10 a.m. to 5 .pm.

Admission Fees
Residenzmuseum 7 Euro
Schatzkammer 7 Euro
Combination Ticket Residenzmuseum/Schatzkammer 11 Euro
Cuvilliés-Theater 3,50 Euro
Entire ticket Residenzmuseum/Schatzkammer/Cuvilliés-Theater 13 Euro
14-day pass 24 Euro
Discounts apply

6.5 Maximilianstrasse

Maximilianstrasse is Munich's most expensive shopping street. Here you find the famous high-end brands with as many designer clothes, gorgeous shoes, glamorous sunglasses, luxurious handbags, stylish writing utensils, classy suitcases, high-end jewelry or expensive watches as you could ever wish for.

Hours
Most shops are open Monday through Saturday 10 a.m. to 8 p.m.
Closed Sundays.

6.6 Meeting Spot and How to Get There

The best meeting spots right on Odeonsplatz are on the stairs of the Feldherrnhalle or at the San Francisco Coffee Company. Both places are great to relax and wait for your friends.

Underground: Lines 3,4,5, and 6 Station Odeonsplatz
Walking: Just a short walk from Marienplatz

6.7 Places to Eat

Café Tambosi at the north end of Odeonsplatz is a great place to see and be seen if you sit outside. But you also should have a glimpse into the nostalgic historic inside. They have a variety of coffee drinks and also nice Italian food.

For a quick snack and free WLAN Internet access go to the **San Francisco Coffee Company** on the west corner of Odeonsplatz.

6.8 Itineraries

Short: Visit Odeonsplatz and Theatinerkirche. Walk through the Hofgarten and admire the Residenz from the outside.

Medium: Visit the crypt in the Theatinerkirche and the one in the Residenz museum.

Long: Visit the complete Residenz, including Cuvilliés Theater and the Treasury, sit down to eat or drink coffee at Café Tambosi. Walk along Maximilianstrasse.

7   Königsplatz

Copyright © OpenStreetMap contributors

The Königsplatz (King's Square) was modeled after the Acropolis in Athens and is the most beautiful classic square in Munich. A wonderful mixture of the ancient world, classicism and modern times.

It indicates the family ties between King Otto of Greece and the Wittelsbacher family in Bavaria. King Ludwig I and his architect Leo van Klenze built it.

Apart from the wide and spacious square, which is an attraction itself, the Königsplatz has three major sights: Propyläen, Glyptothek and the National Collection of Antiques.

But the Königsplatz is also a place for several cultural activities in summer such as the Open Air Cinema or concerts.

31

7.1 Propyläen

Coming from the west on Brienner Street, one of the first boulevards in Munich, you enter the Königsplatz through the Doric Propyläen.

Leo von Klenze built the columns starting in 1817 and are an exact copy of the famous columns in Athens, Greece. Pedestrians can enter them and admire the solid temple-like columns as well as the richly decorated ceiling. Brienner Street circles the Propyläen on both sides, so be careful when passing.

7.2 Glyptothek

The Ionic Glyptothek is the most renowned museum for Greek and Roman sculptures in Europe.

Sculptures in niches adorn the exterior walls, which have no windows at all. The light comes from the windows facing the interior courtyard.

The sculptures represent mythical or historical beings. On the front façade these are Daedalus, Prometheus, Hadrian, Pericles, Phidias and Hephaestus.

Originally built out of marble, the museum was partially destroyed during World War II. The damage was mostly outside, but the reconstruction didn't copy the original.

The collections include world-famous originals as well as Roman copies of Greek masterpieces. The statue of Diomedes, the picture of Homer, the Barberini Faun or the busts of Marius and Sulla are some of the most famous pieces.

Hours
Tuesday through Sunday from 10 a.m. to 5 p.m.
Wednesday 10 a.m. to 8 p.m.
Closed December 24, December 31, Faschingsdienstag (Shrove Tuesday, part Easter week) and Good Friday

Admission Fee
Adults 3,50 Euro
Sunday 1 Euro
Discounts apply

Combination Ticket Glyptothek and National Collection of Antiques 5,50 Euro

7.3 *National Collection of Antiques*

Facing the Glyptothek is the National Collection of Antiques, built after the model of a Corinthian temple. It's one of the biggest collections of antiquities in Germany.

It exhibits vases, bronzes and other artifacts of Greek and Roman life. Frequent temporary exhibitions enhance the museum's permanent exhibition.

Hours
Tuesday through Sunday 10 a.m. to 5 p.m.
Thursday 10 a.m. to 8 p.m.
Closed December 24, December 31 and Faschingsdienstag (Shrove Tuesday, part of Easter week)

Admission Fee
Adults 3,50 Euro
Sunday 1 Euro
Discounts apply
Combination Ticket Glyptothek and National Collection of Antiques 5,50 Euro

7.4 Kunstbau Munich

There are two more attractions at the Königsplatz hidden in the underground: the underground station of the U2 line at Königsplatz is a beautiful station decorated with statues and other artifacts from the Glyptothek and the National Collection of Antiques. Even if you don't travel by public transport, go down and admire the station.

Inside the station on the mezzanine floor is another museum: the Kunstbau München in the Lenbachhaus, an art gallery. After building the underground station, there was unused space and in 1994 it became an exhibition hall. Big windows facing the escalators to the station, which is definitely an extravagant idea, replaced the walls. Now, every underground traveler can glimpse into the art gallery.

7.5 NS Documentation Center

During World War II the then-named Königlicher Platz (Royal Square) was the headquarters of the NSDAP, the National Socialist German Workers' Party (Nazis). After the war the authorities restored the heavily destroyed square to its original condition.

The documentation center is currently under construction and set for inauguration by the end of 2014. It's an educational center to highlight the NS history and its consequences for Munich.

Constructed on the grounds of the former Braunes Haus (brown house), it was the NSDAP's central office.

7.6 Meeting Spot and How to Get There

Meet under the Propyläen or on the stairs of either the Glyptothek or the National Collection of Antiques.

Underground: Line 2 Station Königsplatz
Walking: Just a short walk from Odeonsplatz along Brienner Strasse

7.7 Places to Eat

There's no place to eat at or near the Königsplatz, except for the museum cafeterias. Bring your own food for a picnic on the lawn.

If you walk a few minutes the Briennerstrasse to the West, you arrive at the Löwenbräukeller, Nymphenburger Straße 2, www.loewenbraeukeller.com

Löwenbräu is one of the traditional Munich breweries and they offer authentic Bavarian food and beer. In summer the beer garden is the perfect place to go, on cold days visit the restaurant inside.

7.8 Itineraries

Short: Walk through the Propyläen and enjoy the fantastic Mediterranean feeling on Königsplatz. Visit the underground station.

Medium: Visit the Glyptothek or the National Collections of Antiques.

Long: Visit both museums and the gallery in the Lenbachhaus. Then, relax and have a picnic on the lawn.

8 Kunstareal: Pinakotheken

Copyright © OpenStreetMap contributors

Kunstareal is a relatively new name for the area between the art galleries (Pinakothek) and the Königsplatz. I have put the Königsplatz with its nearby museums as a separate sight just because it's so big.

Munich has three municipal Pinakotheken (art galleries), and they're all within walking distance from each other.

8.1 Alte Pinakothek (Old Pinakothek)

The Alte Pinakothek shows more than 800 masterpieces of European paintings from the 14th to 18th century. It's one of the oldest and most important galleries in the world.

Some of the most important paintings exhibited are:
- The Rubens collection: Let the Rubens Hall with six-meter-high paintings capture you.
- See the self-portrait of Albrecht Dürer and his world-renowned Four Apostles.
- View Rembrandt's self-portrait.
- Other painters in the collection are Altdorfer, Cranach, Botticelli, da Vinci, Raphael, and Titian.

Apart from the permanent exhibitions there are always temporary exhibitions of European painters. When entering the museum, you'll receive an audio guide in several languages. However, the museum also offers guided tours, either to the complete Pinakothek, or just for one painter. Please visit the website for tour schedules. http://www.pinakothek.de/alte-pinakothek/

Even if you're not very interested in art and paintings, have a look at the Alte Pinakothek, at least from the outside. Leo van Klenze under King Ludwig I built it. The king wanted to make his big arts collection available to the public, and he ordered Klenze to build an appropriate home for the paintings.

Construction was finished in 1836 and made the Alte Pinakothek the biggest museum in the world. It soon became an example for many other museums like the Hermitage in St. Petersburg, Russia.

If you decide to enter the Alte Pinakothek, you first arrive in the big entry hall that's as elegant as it is functional. With innovative roof lights the whole hall bursts with light.

During WW II the Allies heavily bombed the building. Fortunately, the paintings had been evacuated beforehand so there were no losses. The museum decided to repair the building only and not to reconstruct. Still today, you can see the bomb damage in the south façade of the building.

Hours
Tuesday 10 a.m. to 8 p.m. Monday closed.
Wednesday through Sunday 10 a.m. to 6 p.m.
Closed on Faschingsdienstag (Shrove Tuesday, a part of Easter week), January 5, December 24 and 25, December 31

Admission Fee
Adults 7 Euro
Sunday 1 Euro
Day pass 12 Euro (all three Pinakotheken, Museum Brandhorst, Sammlung Schack)
Discounts apply

8.2   Neue Pinakothek (New Pinakothek)

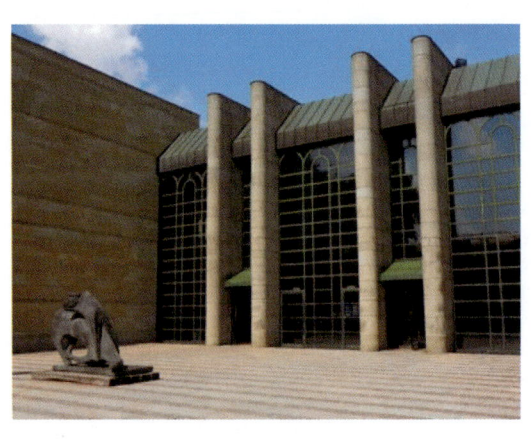

The Neue Pinakothek is "new" compared with the Alte Pinakothek. It features European art and sculpture from the 19th century. The main focus is German art, going back to the private collection of King Ludwig I. But there's also a magnificent collection of French impressionists and Spanish painters.

Famous painters exhibited are:
- Caspar David Friedrich
- Hans von Marées
- Claude Monet
- Edouard Manet
- Francisco Goya
- Edgar Degas
- Pierre-Auguste Renoir
- Paul Cézanne
- Paul Gauguin
- Vincent Van Gogh and his sunflower painting

The new Pinakothek opened in 1853 and was the first and only collection of modern art at that time (not modern now, but it was back then).
The Allies destroyed the building during WW II, and eventually it was demolished and rebuilt from scratch. Alexander Freiherr von Brancas designed the postmodern building, and it opened in 1981.
The outside is still reason for debate among locals, but everyone seems to be enthusiastic about the inside. The clever tour guides you in the form of an eight through the exhibitions in chronological order until you arrive again in the entrance hall without ever crossing one path twice.
The museum offers audio guides as well as guided tours. Please check the website for schedules. http://www.pinakothek.de/neue-pinakothek

Hours
Wednesday 10 a.m. to 8 p.m.
Thursday to Monday 10 a.m. to 6 p.m.
Closed Tuesdays
Closed January 5, December 24 and 25, December 31

Note: This is probably the only city-owned museum that is open on Mondays, but closed on Tuesdays.

Admission Fee
Adults 7 Euro
Sunday 1 Euro
Day pass 12 Euro (all three Pinakotheken, Museum Brandhorst, Sammlung Schack)
Discounts apply

8.3 Pinakothek der Moderne (Pinakothek of Modern Art)

This newest Pinakothek opened its doors in 2002. It's the biggest museum for modern art in Germany. The main focus is art of the 20th and 21st centuries, divided into four separate museums.

1. Modern art collection
This collection features contemporary art and modern art, including expressionism, cubism, Bauhaus, surrealism, and pop art. In addition to paintings you'll find photography, video and new media.

2. State-owned graphic arts collection
More than 350,000 printed graphics and 45,000 master illustrations are here. The Staatliche Graphische Sammlung is one of the most important collections in the world. The graphics range from the 15th century to the present.

3. Design: Die neue Sammlung
The new collection is supposed to be the first museum for design worldwide. It opened in 1925, when even the concept "design" as we use it nowadays didn't exist yet.
Cars, computers, furniture, clothing and even mobile phones are here.

4. Architecture museum
This is part of the Technical University Munich and features a collection of more than half a million architectural illustrations from more than 700 architects as well as photographs and models.

The building itself is a piece of modern art: made of unadorned concrete and a 25-meter- high glass dome. From the spacious entry hall you start to tour the four different areas.

Hours
Tuesday through Sunday 10 a.m. to 6 p.m.
Thursday 10 a.m. to 8 p.m.
Closed Mondays
Closed on Faschingsdienstag (Shrove Tuesday, a part of Easter week), January 5, December 24, 25, 31

Admission Fee
Adults   10 Euro
Sunday   1 Euro
Day pass   12 Euro (all three Pinakotheken, Museum Brandhorst, Sammlung Schack)
Discounts apply.

8.4   Museum Brandhorst

Museum Brandhorst opened to the public in 2009. Udo and Anette Brandhorst (thus the name of the museum) donated this collection of modern art.

Berlin architect Sauerbruch Hutton built the building, and it's an attraction itself. The outer façade is made of 36,000 ceramic poles in 23 colors. Walk by slowly and see how the material and colors seem to change as you pass by.

The permanent exhibit shows the works of Andy Warhol, Damien Hirst, Pablo Picasso, Sigmar Polke and Cy Twombly among others. The Andy Warhol collection is one of the biggest in Europe.
Temporary exhibitions of other famous contemporary artists are frequently on display.

Hours
Tuesday to Sunday 10 a.m. to 6 p.m.
Thursday 10 a.m. to 8 p.m.
Closed Mondays
Closed on Faschingsdienstag (Shrove Tuesday, a part of Easter week), January 5, December 24, 25 and 31

Admission Fee
Adults   7 Euro
Sunday 1 Euro
Day pass   12 Euro (all three Pinakotheken, Museum Brandhorst, Sammlung Schack)
Discounts apply.

8.5 Meeting Spots and How to Get There

Meet in front of the museum you want to visit. Most of them have stairs where you can sit and relax.
Underground: Line U2 Station Theresienstrasse or Königsplatz
Tram: Line 27, Stop Pinakotheken
Bus: Line 154 Stop Schellingstrasse or Line 100 (Museumline) Stops Pinakotheken and Sammlung Brandhorst
Walking: Just a short walk from Königsplatz

8.6 Places to Eat

Apart from the cafés inside each of the museums, there are some great places to go. This is the area where you'll find dozens if not hundreds of restaurants. It's one of the busiest areas in Munich, and the university is here also, so you find quite a few cheap lunch places.
These are two of my favorite restaurants:

Tresznijewski
Theresienstrasse 72, http://www.tresznjewski.com/
Even though you can go there any time of the day, the most enjoyable times are for brunch or a late night drink. They have fantastic breakfasts at a reasonable price. In the evening it's usually very crowded.

Steinheil 16
Steinheilstr 16, +49 89 527488, (no website)
This is a very popular place among students and hungry people. They serve the biggest schnitzel I've ever seen. It's bigger than the plate, and you need to search for the French fries underneath the schnitzel. The chili con carne is another house specialty.

8.7 Itineraries

Short: Take a walk around the quarter, view all the museums from the outside and enter the entrance halls. Visit the one museum you like most.

Medium: Visit one more museum.

Long: Visit all four and take a guided tour.

9 Olmypiapark

Copyright © OpenStreetMap contributors

The Olympic Park in Munich is not only a park with beautifully shaped landscapes, including an artificial hill with a panoramic view and a lake. During its more than 40-year existence it has also become one of most important sites for sports and leisure time events in the city.

Built for the **Olympic Games in 1972**, the Olympic Park in Munich is still popular with tourists as well as locals.

The impressive architecture of the Olympic stadium and the Olympic halls was futuristic 40 years ago and still keeps up with the times today.

The two Olympic halls host such various events as big German companies' shareholder's meetings, trade fairs and indoors concerts.
The landmark tent-style roofs are quite impressive. After the Olympic games the whole venue became a recreation center for Munich. Some of the venues such as the Olympic swimming pool are still in use.

9.1 Television Tower and Rock Museum

You can ascend the Olympic television tower via lift (elevator), to have the most stunning panoramic view of Munich. Even in somewhat foggy weather, the sight is spectacular. At 291 meters it's the highest place in Munich.

On clear days, especially during Föhn (a warm wind coming from Italy), you can see the Alps as big and impressive as if they were just around the corner.

Upstairs on the glass-covered platform is a small **rock 'n' roll museum; the** entrance fee is part of the elevator ticket. This is interesting not only for rock fans. Signed guitars from Frank Zappa, Pink Floyd, ZZ Top, Bruce Springsteen, the Rolling Stones, Kiss, Sting, Queen and others are some of the main attractions. You also find rare vinyl records, gold records, musicians' stage clothes, tickets to concerts, photos and letters from stars and many autographs.

There's a revolving restaurant upstairs, the panorama is spectacular, the food ok, but very pricey.

Hours
Daily 9 a.m. to midnight

Admission Fee
Adults   5 Euro
Under 16:   3,50 Euro

9.2 Olympiastadion

The Olympic stadium is the heart and center of Olympiapark. The big **Olympic stadium** with a maximum capacity of 75,000 people used to be the biggest stadium in Munich and was the home of the famous Bayern Munich Soccer Team.

In 2006 just in time for the Football [soccer] World Cup in Germany, a new and even bigger stadium, the **Allianz arena**, opened. Since then the Olympic stadium doesn't host football matches anymore, but various other sports events and many open-air rock and pop concerts.

Since 2012 there's an exposition about the 1972 Olympic games, explaining the complete process from the application, the preparation and construction until the actual event. The exhibit is in Block M.
At the Besuchereingang Nord (entrance North), there's a 20-minute film shown about the Olympic games.
You can visit the Olympic stadium on your own with an audio guide.

Hours
Daily except when events take place.
Summer   9 a.m. to 6 p.m.
Winter   9 a.m. to 4 p.m.

Admission Fee
Adults   3 Euro
Under 16   2 Euro

There are also guided tours available, and if you're adventurous, go for an exhilarating tour across the rooftops (see picture above) with a 200m Flying Fox descent. http://www.olympiapark.de/en/home/tours-sightseeing/guided-tours/

9.3 Walk of Stars

The Walk of Fame in Hollywood inspired the walk of stars. Along the shore of the Olympic lake you can see the handprints and signatures of famous sports, music and entertainment stars such as Anastacia, Maria Riesch, Ozzy Osbourne, Henry Maske, Supertramp, Scorpions, Michael Stich, Elton John, and the Soccer World Champion Team of 1974.
The requirement to receive a star is to have celebrated a sports success or given a concert in the Olympic Park.

9.4 Tourist Train

A little train runs every day from April to October from 10 a.m. to 6 p.m. (except on days with outdoors events). The tour takes about 20 minutes and gives you a fast overview of all the attractions at the Olmypiapark.

Admission Fee
Adults: 3 Euro
Under 16:   2 Euro

9.5 Meeting Spot and How to Get There

Either you meet at the underground station or in front of the television tower. Underground Line 3 Station Olympiazentrum (not to be confused with Olympiaeinkaufszentrum on the same line, which is a shopping mall)

9.6 Places to Eat

Apart from the high-priced revolving restaurant on top of the television tower, there's also a self-service restaurant at the foot of the tower, which offers good prices, and you can sit outside to enjoy the sunshine.
During festivals there are food stalls everywhere.

9.7 Itineraries

Short: Walk the most important sights or take a tour with the train.

Medium: Visit the television tower and the rock museum.

Long: Visit the stadium and take one of the guided tours.

10 BMW Experience Park

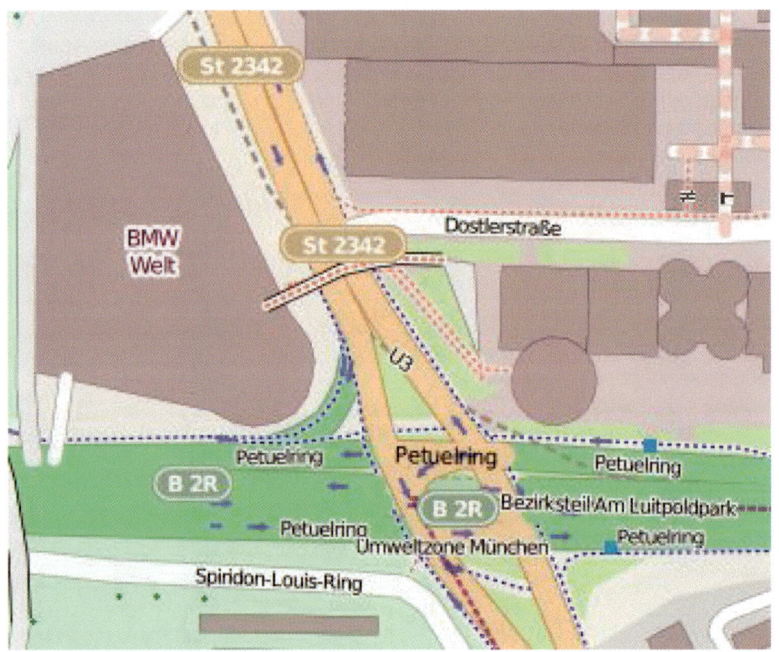

Copyright © OpenStreetMap contributors

The international BMW headquarters are located in Munich near the Olympiapark. The headquarters building and the attached museum, built in 1972 just in time for the Olympic Games, received landmark status several years ago.

Munich residents nicknamed the building **Four-Cylinder** due to its shape, which resembles the cylinders of an engine. After Volkswagen built the Autostadt (city of cars) in Wolfsburg, the other big German automobile manufacturers had to catch up with VW and build their own exhibition worlds.

So, the BMW experience park, inaugurated in October 2007, consists of three parts:

BMW World
BMW Munich Plant
BMW Museum

All three parts connect via a bridge.

46

10.1 BMW Welt – BMW World

The main reason for the double cone building is to welcome car buyers who want to pick up their new cars personally and make the exchange as exciting as possible.

But even for non-buyers there's a lot to see. The futuristic building itself is worth looking at, and it hosts several highlights such as a turning platform with the newest automobile models. It also has museum-like educational exhibits with buttons to push, and even a driving simulator rounds off the experience.

If you're even remotely interested in cars, this is a must-see attraction in Munich. It shows the world's **largest permanent BMW automobile exhibition.** Some of the highlights are Formula 1 racing cars, a collection of luxury Rolls-Royces and an entire exhibition dedicated to the future of mobility with electric and hydrogen cars. On the second floor you can even mount several BMW motorbikes.

Hours
Daily 7:30 a.m. until midnight (Exhibits are only open until 6 p.m.)
Closed December 24, 25, 26, 31 and January 1.

Admission Free

10.2 BMW Plant – Guided Tour

There's still a working plant right here at the international BMW headquarters. It produces more than 1400 motors and 900 cars daily. Wow!
It's one of the most modern car factories worldwide, and you can get a glimpse into it during one of the guided tours.
The tour takes two–and-a-half hours.

Admission Fee
Adults   8 Euro
Under 18   5 Euro
Languages are German and English.

Hours
Monday through Friday 9 a.m. to 4:30 p.m.
You must book your desired dates well in advance via phone or email.
Tel.: 089 1250 160 01
Fax: 089 1250 160 09   email: infowelt@bmw-welt.com

10.3 BMW Museum

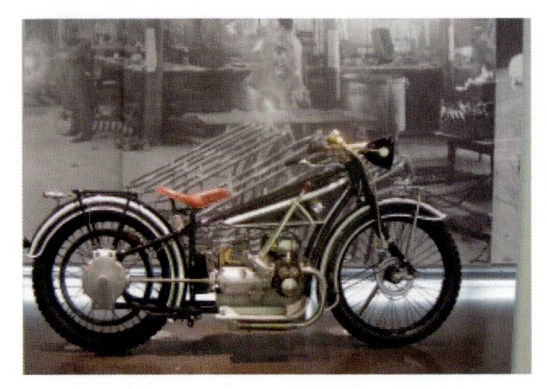

The BMW Museum is fascinating, not only for car fanatics, but for anyone remotely interested in the history of automobiles. It's now totally revamped and reopened its doors in 2008 with a very modern and entertaining exhibit. Not the usual, old, boring museum you might expect.

You start the tour with a surprising design study of a BMW, made out of LED lights.
This "spectacle" sets the tone for the rest of the exhibit. BMW works with unusual and modern concepts of light, sound and interactivity. The cars are in some parts of the museum only, a nice side activity.

Despite the modern spirit, history plays a big part as well. From the first BMW motorcycles to beautiful old-timers and the world-famous Isetta, there's a lot to see from more than 90 years of BMW company existence.

If you're more interested in the technology behind the scenes, you'll delight in the House of Technology. It features engines as well as the themes "aerodynamics" and "lightweight construction." Admire the famous BMW six-cylinder engine, as well as several aircraft engines.

There's also a complete exhibition dedicated to motorsports. BMW's successes in motor racing date back to the 1930s.

Hours
Tuesday through Sunday 10 a.m. to 6 p.m.
Cosed Mondays
Closed: December 24, 25, 26, 31, January 1

Note: Due to an event the museum is closed October 16, 2013.

Admission Fee
Adults   9 Euro
Under 18:   6 Euro

10.4 Meeting Spot and How to Get There

Meet in front of the museum or at the side entrance (the one facing the underground station) of the BMW World.
Underground Line 3 Station Olympiazentrum (not to be confused with Olympiaeinkaufszentrum on the same line, which is a shopping mall)

Walking: A short walking distance from Olympiapark

10.5 Places to Eat

There's a café in the BMW Museum and one in the BMW World. Both are the typical museum cafés. If you're really hungry, there's a Pizza Hut on the corner just across Petuelring.
Unfortunately there are no nice restaurants nearby.

10.6 Itineraries

Short: Visit BMW World.

Medium: Visit the BMW museum as well.

Long: Take a guided plant tour.

11 Nymphenburg Castle

Copyright © OpenStreetMap contributors

Bavarian kings and dukes **built Nymphenburg Palace** (also called Nymphenburg Castle) in 1664 as their summer residence. In the 17th century Munich was still a tiny village, not much bigger than the area from Stachus (Karlsplatz) to Marienplatz.
Nymphenburg was pure "countryside," far away from the hassles of the capital. It would take almost half a day to get there either by walking or by horse coach. Nowadays, Munich is much bigger, and Nymphenburg Palace lies almost in the heart of the city. You can reach it easily in 15 to 20 minutes with Tram 17 from Hauptbahnhof (central station).

The 10-minute walk from the tram station along the **Auffahrtsallee** toward the palace is simply amazing. You walk along an artificial water channel and green pastures with blossoming flowers until you finally reach the breathtaking baroque main building with its huge side buildings.

Museum Hours
April to October 15   9 a.m. – 6 p.m.
October 16 to March   10 a.m. – 4 p.m.

Closed: January 1, Shrove Tuesday, (a part of Easter week), Dec 24, 25, 31

Admission Fee
Combination ticket Nymphenburg
Summer: 11.50 Euro regular / 9 Euro reduced
Winter: 8.50 Euro regular / 6.50 Euro reduced
Valid for Main Palace, Marstallmuseum, Museum of Nymphenburg Porcelain and the park palaces. In winter the park palaces are closed.

Nymphenburg Palace: 6 Euro regular/5 Euro reduced
Museums or Parkburgen (park palaces): 4.50 Euro regular / 3.50 Euro reduced

11.1 Nymphenburg Main Palace

The main palace is huge and has 21 rooms open to visitors. To get the most out of your visit, use an audio guide because there are no guided tours available. The tour starts at the overwhelming Main Hall and continues through several richly decorated antechambers, bedrooms and cabinets, and galleries.
Some of the highlights include:
Elector Max Emanuel's Great Gallery of Beauties with paintings of court ladies. Paintings of the different building projects Max Emanuel started line the North Gallery, which he used as a ceremonial entry into his apartment.

Most famous is probably King Ludwig I's Gallery of Beauties. It consisted of 36 portraits of beautiful women of all social classes that Joseph Stieler painted. The best known are the "Schöne Münchnerin" (the Beauty of Munich) Helene Sedlmayr, daughter of a shoemaker, and the "Spanish" dancer Lola Montez, cause of the revolution in 1848, when Ludwig I had to abdicate.
And last but not least, Queen Caroline's bedroom where on August 25, 1845 the Crown Princess Marie gave birth to the baby who would become King Ludwig II.

11.2 Gardens and Park

Many habitants from Munich visit Nymphenburg Palace gardens to sit on the grass and enjoy themselves.

This is something very special to Munich: As soon as the sun shines (winter or summer!), everyone flocks to the many public parks to be outside with friends and family.

Do it like the locals, bring food and drinks, your favorite book and enjoy the day relaxing!

The park underwent considerable changes from a baroque garden to a landscaped park. Friedrich Ludwig von Sckell is the architect who created this masterpiece of garden design. (He also designed the English garden.) There's a permanent exhibition in the geranium house about the history and concept of the Nymphenburg park. It explains many details such as why the park keepers must remove healthy trees each year to maintain balance in the garden.

The large fountains in the park are much more than a terrific sight to view. They once were the newest in Bavarian technology. Engineer Joseph von Baader installed the pump system in the greenhouse in 1803, and it's the oldest machine in Europe that has worked continuously ever since.
The park covers a total of 229 hectares, and admission is free for all outside areas, including the greenhouse.

Hours

January, February and November: 6:30 a.m. – 6 p.m.
March: 6 a.m. – 6:30 p.m.
April and September: 6 a.m. – 8:30 p.m.
May to August: 6 a.m. – 9:30 p.m.
October: 6 a.m. – 7 p.m.
December: 6:30 a.m. – 5:30 p.m.

Fountains run from Easter to mid-October from 10 a.m. to noon and from 2 p.m. to 4 p.m.

The historic Green Pump House in the Little Village and Johannis Pump House in the north wing of the palace are open daily from 10 a.m. to 4 p.m. from Easter to the beginning of October.

11.3 Park Castles

Nymphenburg Park features four smaller park castles.

1. Amalienburg Hunting Lodge
Elector Karl Albrecht built the small **Amalienburg** from 1734 to 1739 as a hunting lodge for his wife Maria Amalia (therefore the name Amalia's castle).
The single-story building with its unique hall of mirrors decorated partly in silver is a masterpiece of European rococo art.
François Cuvilliés the Elder was responsible for the design. Johann Baptist Zimmermann for the most part did the stuccowork. Johann Joachim Dietrich did the woodcarving, and Joseph Pasqualin Moretti did the painting.
The Hall of Mirrors is definitely the most spectacular of the rooms, but the kitchen's richly decorated Dutch tiles and painted Chinese scenes are amazing.

2. Badenburg

Badenburg means "the house of baths" and as the name says, it was for bathing. The basement accommodates the bath itself, the heating room, the kitchen and some more bathing rooms.
Also a banquet room takes up two floors and a small apartment for the elector.

3. Pavilion Pagodenburg

Joseph Effner built the Pagodenburg between 1716 and 1719. Greens surround the pavilion where the residents used to play a game similar to golf called Mailspiel.

4. Magdalenenklause

Effner built another pavilion also. He conceived it as living quarters for a hermit, and it looks like a ruin from the outside. This was part of the concept. The hermitage was the hiding place for Elector Max Emanuel to escape reality and contemplate.

11.4 Marstallmuseum

The Marstallmuseum in the former royal stables shows a luxurious collection of carriages and sleighs the royal family owned.
It also contains the Nymphenburg porcelain museum, with the famous porcelain collection of the Bäuml family. Since 1986 the porcelain has been on display in the rooms above the carriage and sleigh exhibition.

11.5 Meeting Spot and How to Get There

The best meeting spot is just in front of the main entrance. You can choose sun or shade.
Tram: Line 16 Romanplatz or Line 17 Amalienburgstrasse from Karlsplatz/Stachus to the stop Schloss Nymphenburg.

Note: The walk from the tram stop to the castle takes at least 10 minutes. If you have walking difficulties, use either one of the hop-on/hop-off buses that leave you much nearer to the castle entrance or take a taxi.

11.6 Places to Eat

Schlosswirtschaft zur Schwaige
Schloss Nymphenburg 30, http://www.schlosswirtschaft-schwaige.de/
A nice, but a bit pricey Bavarian restaurant. The atmosphere and the food are good, and it's the nearest place to the castle.

Rotkreuzplatz
Take the tram or bus back to Rotkreuzplatz and chose from the many restaurants here. This is a lively square where lots of locals go out for lunch and dinner.

Sarcletti Ice Cream
Nymphenburger Str. 155
Some say it's the best ice cream parlor in Munich. Well, it must have some truth to it because in summer there's always a long queue at the sidewalk sale.
Extra Tip: go inside and sit at one of the tables, it's usually less crowded.

11.7 Itineraries

Short: Visit the main palace and take a short walk through the park.

Medium: Talk an extended walk through the park and visit the greenhouse.

Long: Visit the Marstallmuseum and some or all of the park palaces

12 About the Author

Marion Kummerow has moved to Munich more than 15 years ago, where she met her future husband during a visit to the Oktoberfest. Since then she has lived in different parts of Munich with her family.
In 2004 she and her husband started the website www.inside-munich.com, in order to show the beauties of Munich to foreign visitors.
She has put all of her knowledge about Munich into this guide book, to help her readers get the best out of their vacation.

Become a Fan on Facebook
 http://www.facebook.com/InsideMunichGuide and never miss an important update.

„To get more tips about Munich, click the link below to subscribe to our newsletter."
inside-munich.com/tips

Also by Marion Kummerow

The Ultimate Guide to Oktoberfest
Everything you need to know about the Oktoberfest in Munich. Includes a detailed description of all beer tents, how to make a reservation and even secret tips on what to do if you don't have a reservation.

German Christmas Traditions
A comprehensive book on German Christmas traditions with very personal views from the author who was born and raised in Germany. Here you find everything you always wanted to know about German Christmas, including four of the best Christmas Cookie recipes and the lyrics to three famous German Christmas Carols.

How to Rent An Apartment in Munich
The detailed step-by-step instructions in How to Rent an Apartment in Munich: Multiply Your Chances to Move into Your Dream Apartment map out your move to Germany for you. The helpful glossary of German words will help you communicate with lessors.

Thank you for purchasing my book. Please review this book on Amazon.
I use your feedback to make the next version better. Thank you so much!

Printed in Great Britain
by Amazon.co.uk, Ltd.,
Marston Gate.